RARE HIGH MEADOW OF WHICH I MIGHT DREAM

RARE HIGH MEADOW OF
WHICH I MIGHT DREAM

CONNIE VOISINE

THE UNIVERSITY OF CHICAGO PRESS

Chicago and London

CONNIE VOISINE is associate professor of English at New
Mexico State University and the author of a book of poems
entitled *Cathedral of the North*, which received the Associated
Writing Program's poetry prize.

Title page illustration: Jacklyn St. Aubyn, *Distraction* (details).
By permission of the artist.

The University of Chicago Press, Chicago 60637
The University of Chicago Press, Ltd., London
© 2008 by The University of Chicago
All rights reserved. Published 2008
Printed in the United States of America
17 16 15 14 13 12 11 10 09 08   1 2 3 4 5

ISBN-13: 978-0-226-86351-1 (cloth)
ISBN-13: 978-0-226-86352-8 (paper)
ISBN-10: 0-226-86351-4 (cloth)
ISBN-10: 0-226-86352-2 (paper)

Library of Congress Cataloging-in-Publication Data
Voisine, Connie.
    Rare high meadow of which I might dream / Connie
    Voisine.
        p. cm. — (Phoenix poets)
    ISBN-13: 978-0-226-86351-1 (alk. paper)
    ISBN-10: 0-226-86351-4 (alk. paper)
    ISBN-13: 978-0-226-86352-8 (pbk. : alk. paper)
    ISBN-10: 0-226-86352-2 (pbk. : alk. paper)
    I. Title.
    PS3622.O37R37 2008
    811'.6—dc22   2007015698

♾ The paper used in this publication meets the minimum
requirements of the American National Standard for
Information Sciences—Permanence of Paper for Printed
Library Materials, ANSI Z39.48-1992.

for Rus

He tried to say no but said slow
and I did as his tongue required.
He wanted wrong but said thorn,
and I rushed to the hedge of those roses.

— SHMUEL HA NAGID

Contents

Acknowledgments · xi

The Early Days of Aviation · 3
The Invisible Man remained · 6
The Bird is Her Reason · 8
Anonymous Lyric · 13
Love Poem · 15
Fly · 17
Dangerous for Girls · 19
Apart, Away · 22
First Taste · 26
WeatherCam—the Horizon · 37
To Ireland, To Bethlehem · 39
The Bitter After · 42
Sorry I Don't Like You · 49
The Beginning of Things · 52
This is for the silver of highway · 55

Notes · 59

Acknowledgments

Grateful acknowledgment is made to the editors of the following magazines where these poems or versions of these poems first appeared:

Ellipsis: "Apart, Away"

The Georgia Review: "This is for the silver of highway." This poem originally appeared in *The Georgia Review*, Volume LVII, Number 2 (Summer 2003), © 2003 by The University of Georgia. Reprinted by permission of *The Georgia Review* and Connie Voisine.

Hunger Mountain: "To Ireland, To Bethlehem," "The Early Days of Aviation," "The Beginning of Things"

POOL: A Journal of Poetry: "The Bird is Her Reason"

Puerto del Sol: "Anonymous Lyric"

Slate (www.slate.com): "Love Poem"

Thanks to From the Fishouse: an online audio archive of emerging poets, www.fishousepoems.org, for archiving recordings of the following poems on the Web: "Sorry I Don't Like You," "Apart, Away," and "The Early Days of Aviation."

I would like to thank the following writers for their fierceness, friendship, and help with these poems: Sheila Black, Robert Boswell, Bobby Byrd, James McMichael, Brenda Miller, Antonya Nelson, Patty Seyburn, and Carmen Giménez-Smith.

RARE HIGH MEADOW OF WHICH I MIGHT DREAM

The Early Days of Aviation

St. Exupéry stayed in the hotel between flights
for the postal service. Then, they navigated by landmarks—
a farmhouse, a body of water—and,
when those were made invisible, a compass,
and flashlight. No wonder he imagined
a prince on a tiny planet
as he hurled himself against the constellations.
The world was a dark scroll unrolling beneath
and the plane could become a vehicle you'd use
the way a gnat uses its wings, with a three-dimensional
fluidity and the world might feel to you
the way water must feel to a dolphin.
It was too cold in that hotel, wind
snaked through the cracked-framed windows
and faded drapes. I was easily distracted—too cold
for too long. I could tell you this was the year that I too
flew through a darkness, but at the time
I only felt ugly, inarticulate. I'd take a hot bath
every other night for 5 extra francs. So hot
I barely breathed for a half-hour
after emerging, my heart still beating hard and fast.
I'd go directly to bed and sleep 10 hours. Too cold

and I wanted the day to pass so I could
start over. In the papers, a man more than eighty years old
named Papon was being tried as a collaborator

for the Nazis. During the trial,
his frail wife died, a result of stress. Papon explained
that he took the papers handed to him by Germans,
signed them, and sent the papers on. This is what
kept him alive, he said, signing these papers
which sent hundreds of French Jews to the gas chambers.
The young Papon was dapper in the wartime
photos, his wife well-shod and I wondered at how
what doesn't happen at its neglected moment
flares up, virulent, more so from regret.
How we are all accountable and how it never stops.
Sometimes, I eavesdropped on the nasal

American couple next door—animated in the hallway,
a key in a lock, and I held my breath. Him, with his athletic
stomach and sideburns talking much and more
than she. They wore the banal uniform of American travelers,
as if they might be forced to tear through a jungle
or conquer a mountain, but nighttime
she wore a rich leather jacket with scalloped details
on the pockets and cuffs. Lying in my creaking,
deep-slung bed, lonely, I imagined speaking
before them. We'd make plans and their casual natures
were very attractive, made me feel at ease. I imagined
sitting at dinner with them—why? In my vision
I was flushed, internal, explaining what it is
to be a writer. That one is constantly revealing oneself.
That, as a result, a writer always needs love
but never can remember being loved enough. I'd wrestle

the pillows and debate turning on the light
to read my textbook about French cathedrals, muttering,
what do I think they can give me?

I would sometimes try to imagine what it would be
to play in the sky.

The medieval builders of cathedrals abandoned
barbaric forms, wrote Georges Duby—the vegetal motifs,
the repetition of abstract designs. They moved toward
grander, more elaborate forms
of worship—gold and splendor, biblical
tales reproduced in whole, hundreds
of angels carved in stone as if making it look
human could dissolve the terror
of mystery. I wondered at barbarism—the combination
of the real, minor vine and leaf with the fathomless,
solid expression of a circle inside a square.
I looked around my hotel room at the strewn
clothing, the chipped sink that leaned from the wall, the crack

in the plaster that looked like a man leaping
over the dresser. I understood that the only thing I wanted
from this world was that it need me. And it
did not—a woman waiting in her bed
because there was nowhere she would go. And weren't those
the fearless, early days of aviation—a plane,
the tiny arrow shooting toward an oblivion of sky, wind,
the spree of flight, the eventual
crumpled metal in a farmer's field?

The Invisible Man remained

invisible. Gloves, sleeves,
           bandages limned

his body but soon he gave that up, scared
                         his friends, moved
    about them the way other people's water
moans through the walls
        in old apartment buildings and hotels.
                Once, she felt
a heat at her back and his wife
        threw her dishpan of water
                        and for a silver moment
        he existed, water sluicing off
the bridge of his nose,
               his hair articulate,
    hanging matted
        like moss,
        his eyelids, his grimace,
            then   a puddle on the kitchen floor,
    an outline of shoes,
and he runs. The small prayer,
        what she repeats   without knowing,
           is how much
she wants
        a clean, pure
    widowhood for herself

not this empty hand
on her neck, the weight
of him at night in their bed and her own twisted body
against vacant space.

The Bird is Her Reason

There are some bodies that emerge
                         into desire as a god
rises from the sea, emotion and
                memory hang like dripping clothes—this
      want is like
                   entering that heated red

on the mouth of a Delacroix lion,
        stalwart, always that red
            which makes
my teeth ache and my skin feel
      a hand that has never touched me,
               the tree groaning outside becomes
        a man who knocks on my bedroom window,
edge of red on gold fur,
        the horse, the wild
flip of its head, the rake of claws
        across its back, the unfocussed,
                swallowed eye.

Here's a story:
        two people, neighbors.
She drives by his house one night, sees him play a fiddle
      in the lit
        window. He visits her husband
          while she listens

from the kitchen—what to do but swipe the already-swiped
        table as their laughter daggers the room.
                You must know
        how, in adulterous love,
                one begins to feel fatal, beautiful. The edges of your body
become a tense meniscus and
        in a kind of pain you fear this love
can only lead to a death—

When the moon caught itself in the net of trees
                at the border of the field
        and her husband was asleep, she often rose,
                put on her robe.

                        Window to window,
the man and she
        watching
                across clipped grass, the beds
                        of silvered ferns,
        window to window, her lover waiting

in his, and her husband asks her
        why she stands there
                restless, hungry, fevered, she
says she can't sleep,
        she must listen

to a bird singing in the yard.
        I think
                of Coleridge's bird, his fluttering stranger,
of Keats's *darkling, I listen . . .*
                I have been half in love
                        with easeful death

and the bird is
　　singing at the time of day when the earth
　　　　is darker than the sky and the grief
of the unlived life.
　　I think the bird is
　　her lover, conceived

as we conceive the one we love,
　　to a plain tune from a fiddle rising,
　　to a lumescence of moon,
　　　　hip to the cool sill.
　　　　　　　　Its body is plain to me,
　　　　　　　　　　head a hood
　　　　　　　　of close feathers, a single eye.
I can hear its feet shake

　　the leaves and the bird is
　　　　my own body, glove-colored, a wild,
open throat.

　　The bird is her reason,
voice unbridling her, the irrigation
　　ditches are flooded, doubling
　　　　stars and the lover,

　　　　　　　　but we see
　　only his shape at the window,
　　the way his hair erases the line

of his neck. Sometimes all we want is one of these
　　Lenten lovers, full of a chaste passion repressed. Through the
　　window
she sees his arms are crossed on his chest

but at some point

he becomes pure figure—his eyes pecked clean, bones a tree
for rags and a bird,
      the woman who is dying at her window. Desire is

a kind of liquid, I am starting to think. It wets
      the ground, soaks the clothes on the line
           and makes the street tar look velvet.
Then it stills
the way water off the roof in winter
      tapers to a cool, barely visible
         point like a needle.

      The way Marie de France finished this story
        is one night, the husband kills
          the bird. The servants
set traps in the chestnut trees, poured birdlime on every branch in their yard,
    and once it is captured,
        he shakes the living
bird in her face, says here is your bird, maybe
            now you can sleep.
She begs, but he breaks its neck,
      flings the body at her. Blood dark on
        her nightgown,

she shrouds the bird in a silk shawl
      embroidered with a letter to her lost
        love and the servant
delivers it next door. Both bird and silk
      he closes
      in a jeweled box, her words
to rot with the body.

I am not sure how I would have finished the story,
except

       I know she believes
       we don't get to choose.

Anonymous Lyric

It was the summer of 1976 when I saw the moon fall down.

It broke like a hen's egg on the sidewalk.

The garden roiled with weeds, hummed with gnats who settled clouds on my

oblivious siblings.

A great hunger insatiate to find /A dulcet ill, an evil sweetness blind.

A gush of yolk and then darker.

Somewhere a streetlamp disclosed the insides of a Chevy Impala—vinyl seats,
the rear-view,

headrests and you, your hand through your hair.

An indistinguishable burning, failing bliss.

Because the earth's core was cooling, all animals felt the urge to wander.

Wash down this whisper of you, the terrible must.

Maybe the core wasn't cooling, but I felt a coolness in my mother.

That girl was shining me on.

In blue crayon, the bug-bitten siblings printed lyrics on the walls of my room.

I wrote the word LAVA on my jeans.

It must be the Night Fever, I sang with the 8-track.

But the moon had not broken on the sidewalk, the moon

was hot, bright as a teakettle whistling outside my door,

tied up in sorrow, lost in my song, if you don't come back . . .

and that serious night cooled, settling like sugar on our lawn.

I wrote the word SUGAR on my palms.

I shall say what inordinate love is.

The moon rose itself up on its elbows and shook out its long hair.

Love Poem

Although the angels of numbers and letters
wrestle darkness into shapes, and the plane
descending over the I-10 wraps

my car in the gust and sonic draw of velocity—
it too has a flight path and calm passengers and no
fiery end for us—I duck and think, *so this is it*.

Medievals thought hunger lived its own life in the
body, parasitic, our organs entered by it.
Love was like this too, a contagion, the blood-

filled heart unlocked by his face, her voice,
and we suffered from its side effects of hedonism,
forgetting. The geranium on my porch seems to be

a testament to the finite, the stable, in the warp
of its knobby stems and the slip of white
at each petal's seat, 99 cents at Kmart, but lush

hairs blur the edges of leaves and its musk
supercedes—the water I drink standing near it tastes
heavy and spiced. This flower unlocks, hunger-like,

borders (my mouth, my nose, the water) as does the 747.
Overfull, virulent, the plane dissolves the differences
between my arms, the steering wheel, the airport's

sky and fills me with a roaring which Medievals
could only see as dangerous. Animals
killed for slaughter spill their hunger, see how they

continue to bite at the earth? They believed this pour
was absorbed by the grasses and trees, geraniums,
air, and see how much and why I lose myself to you.

Fly

Wings so fast they are lava,
her small adolescent body
pinched between them. She is

an elevator without the cage of a
shaft, without the hospital or multiplex

office building, up, down, backwards.
Sometimes she is pure
reverie. The yodeling of wind, the purple thistle,
the jackrabbit of a memory

of paler light, axle grease in its cut,
a rotting crow by the road.
Sometimes she is

pure flesh: the dizzy swoop
of the yard to stop against a cool window.
Up close she's plush
across her torso with

arched ankles, hooked feet, she can
walk up anything—the walls, the ceiling.

An organ descends, tubed,
probing, gentle, her mouth, and soon she
tastes the boy's body, ready
coals, the tree by the river,

liquor of night and the swell of moss
beneath it, the events that will stop her in their web,
force the first
failure, pain.
But eventually she will

start up again, her wings
quivering with a voice
high and inconsistent.

Dangerous for Girls

It was the summer of Chandra Levy, disappearing
      from Washington, D.C., her lover a Congressman, evasive
            and blow-dried from Modesto, the TV wondering

in every room in America to an image of her tight jeans and piles
      of curls frozen in a studio pose. It was the summer the only
            woman known as a serial killer, a ten-dollar whore trolling

the plains of central Florida, said she knew she would
      kill again, murder filled her dreams
            and if she walked in the world, it would crack

her open with its awful wings. It was the summer that in Texas, another
      young woman killed her five children, left with too many
            little boys, always pregnant. One Thanksgiving, she tried

to slash her own throat. That summer the Congressman
      lied again about the nature of his relations, or,
            as he said, he couldn't remember if they had sex that last

night he saw her, but there were many anonymous girls that summer,
      there always are, who lower their necks to the stone
            and pray, not to God but to the Virgin, herself once

a young girl, chosen in her room by an archangel.
        Instead of praying, that summer I watched television, reruns of
                a UFO series featuring a melancholic woman detective

who had gotten cancer and was made sterile by aliens. I watched
        infomercials: exercise machines, pasta makers,
                and a product called Nails Again With Henna,

ladies, make your nails steely strong, <u>naturally,</u>
        and then the photograph of Chandra Levy
                would appear again, below a bright red number,

such as 81, to indicate the days she was missing.
        Her mother said, *please understand how we're feeling*
                when told that the police don't believe she will be found alive,

though they searched the parks and forests
        of the Capitol for remains and I remembered
                being caught in Tennessee, my tent filled with wind

lifting around me, *tornado honey*, said the operator when I called
        in fear. The highway barren, I drove to a truck stop where
                maybe a hundred trucks hummed in pale, even rows

like eggs in a carton. Truckers paced in the dining room,
        fatigue in their beards, in their bottomless
                cups of coffee. The store sold handcuffs, dirty

magazines, t-shirts that read, *Ass, gas or grass.*
        Nobody rides for free, and a bulletin board bore a
                public notice: *Jane Doe, found in refrigerator box*

outside Johnson, *TN*, her slight measurements and weight.
  The photographs were of her face, not peaceful in death,
    and of her tattoos *Born to Run*, and *J.T.* caught in

scrollworks of roses. One winter in Harvard Square, I wandered
  drunk, my arms full of still warm, stolen laundry, and
    a man said, *come to my studio* and of course I went—

for some girls, our bodies are not immortal so much as
  expendable, we have punished them or wearied
    from dragging them around for so long and so we go

wearing the brilliant plumage of the possibly freed
  by death. Quick on the icy sidewalks, I felt thin and
    fleet, and the night made me feel unique in the eyes

of the stranger. He told me he made sculptures
  of figure skaters, not of the women's bodies,
    but of the air that whipped around them,

a study of negative space,
  which he said was the where-we-were-not
    that made us. Dizzy from beer,

I thought, *why not step into*
  that space? He locked the door behind me.

Apart, Away

I lived in somebody else's
     holy city,
               and this was the truth—
pilgrims wandered in their suits   and hose dazzled
                      by blue mountains,
      numerous plain monuments to holy things
I did not believe were real.
       I lived
          with a man, kind, but too sad to be
            of consolation. I remember
            the edge
of his face,
     his back, a birth mark
        in the shape of a ghost and the funnel of each day, of walking
after a storm
     with the rent check, snow in blunt banks
against the ecstatic,
        emptied sky, the sidewalks
        warmed
        by salt.

Some nights on my porch,
               I'd look up—
                  at what? Things beyond
     words. Stars
monotone in their beyondness.

Synecdoche without
referent. Smug cold grit. The part
that knows
how to stand for a whole—for something like infinity.

I could not bear that scale.

* * *

Banished for loving his uncle's wife, Tristan entered
                                        exile

        and separation filled his lover Isolde
like a black stain. She
                did not wash, forgot
how to speak except for her
                        rumbles of doubt,
the boom of her solitude. You know this decay, how the body becomes
                        a clot of expendable
        cells,
                anvil
                        or socket
        and in a wildness of
not caring, you
        walk home at 2 am and
                fall into a gun at the gut,
                        a broken
                zipper is what you raise your eyes from to say,
I don't have anything.

* * *

The stars were thick
and the Milky Way   a pale ravine
          over my head. Moon Lake because it was cold

and round
and white.
Mules and horses
          waited at a fence
and the muscular bay I worried for—he

          had freed himself from the pen but remained near the others,
cropping the clover
          on the other side. I could hear
the grinding of his teeth. A great
          horned owl's   wings rattled
an empty cedar
          and suddenly

a crowd of mule deer was
so near I could smell
          their heat, the oil in their fur. I tell you
          this is the truer ending—how

they calmly crossed the threshold
          on thin legs and tiny feet,
          stepped through,
                    apart, away,
too many to count, unintelligible,
          into the black snarl of trees.

First Taste

When you are twenty, walk to the bedside
of the second classmate who attempts suicide
that fall. Walk past Linsly-Chittenden,

Old Campus, to the hospital. Yale's stony
Gothic buildings mark an edge. Cross Crown Street,
walk a nether zone of warehouses, highway

overpasses and the occasional, forlorn storefront. Feel
the severe opulence of the campus and the poverty
of the city in your bones. The sadness of the ice cream shop

in the December half-light of 4 p.m. George,
the friend, has taken a bottle of Extra-Strength Tylenol
during exam week after he is rejected by a friend.

The ambulance driver told him only 7 are necessary
to kill the liver and then one is less likely to vomit them up.
File away the knowledge. With his square block of a body,

strong arms and one of those pretty Protestant faces,
George can present his desperate act with an elegant,
well-bred humor with which you are infatuated. In the solarium,

the place where people can smoke, he crosses his legs slowly,
gestures towards the windowless walls. *Solarium*, he says.
And you laugh. You smoke too, try not to look concerned.

George says the doctors test him daily. Voices, sense of self,
inkblots for Christ's sake. He has to do this so they will release him
in time for Christmas. But this is not the hard part for George.

This is before miracle drugs like Prozac, before smoking is illegal
in public spaces, before you, George, and most of your friends,
know grief is something you can pass through.

2.

You will never be so lonely as you are that first year
in New York City. You sublet an apartment
with a daycare worker on the Upper West Side.

You live in a curtained-off alcove of the living room of the
small, dark one-bedroom on 99th Street. You work at a school
with much older women, and each way, a long subway ride—

the train shoots up out of the ground for the last ten stops,
over warehouses, endless parking lots full of busses, and
meat warehouses by the river. All the way there, you nibble

a donut and sip coffee to stay awake as you chug against
the traffic to that outer borough. The downtown train rushes
past too close, full of men and women crammed together, hanging

on the straps, leaning against the doors, falling on each other
as their train hurtles south. On your uptown train,
you always get a seat. Terrified of falling asleep, you think

someone might slip something awful into your slackened mouth.
But you must have closed your eyes. The Italian anisette
from the cookie factory perfumes

the nearly empty car. Just a couple more stops.
You meet one new friend that winter, a friend suggests
you call her. Elise is a native New Yorker and proud of it

in that rustic, narrow way New Yorkers have. She lives
with her mother in a large, rent-controlled apartment
about 20 blocks south of yours and tells you in your first phone call

she has over 70 pairs of shoes, no small effort since her feet
are unusually narrow and long. She is the first you meet
who refers to herself in other than first person. She talks about

her comfortable life. She tells you about her immigrant boyfriend
who goes to Columbia, his family, how much they love her.
How she goes to Hunter and is saving her money for law school.

Many times that night and during many dinners afterward,
you hear her announce what type of a person she is. She describes
all her qualities to you and you listen, hypnotized by her self-

involvement. You want to understand what it means
not to suffer. You are beginning to learn you had a different
kind of childhood, and the shock is only starting to sink in

so you see suffering everywhere. People
you don't even know tell you their troubles; each woman
at your school has her own well of sorrow. One has a child

who will eat $200 of groceries a night so she can throw it up.
One has breast cancer, another has a severely disabled
adult child. The subway is a study hall of suffering.

You watch and intuit, read faces, bodies with your high-
powered lens of pain. And the skateboard man,
legless with bulging shoulders and arms,

rolling down the subway car, and the man with eye sockets
of scars, but even the ruined shoes of the man reading
a bible in a home-sewn case can make you feel like sobbing.

Elise becomes the stay against the knowledge that everyone,
rich or poor, suffers. Years later, you hear an odd rumor about her.
She did go to law school and there she began to be "sick" often.

When her illnesses were questioned by her professors,
she told them she had AIDS. They eventually required
documentation. Elise is either being sued, the friend said,

or is negotiating a settlement with the university for her deception.
It is a long time before you can feel pity for her, a pretender,
a betrayer of what you believed her to be, simple and lucky.

3.

One night that first fall in New York, you go to see
Geraldine Ferraro, listen to her through the loudspeakers
set up on the sidewalk because a woman

has been nominated. For her, you have been stapling democratic
materials at the headquarters. The idea of her is bright
that fall, though hers is a losing campaign and we all

know it. All kinds of women stand on the sidewalk
with you. It's cold and most are still in work clothes
with uncomfortable office shoes. A group of teenaged girls

pour from a church bus, meander through the crowd.
You feel a beautiful, fatalistic hope and
lost, on a wide, open-air platform in the south Bronx,

you wait for a train. The buildings
are burned or have grates or scrap metal over windows
or window-gaps. Men and women

stagger in and out of the station, thin enough
to slip through the turnstiles without the ease of a token.
They have white lips, knotted hair and their clothes

are irrelevant to them. These people are persistent, plead
with you while other passengers stare straight ahead.
You can't bear such naked need. It makes you feel ashamed, you

who walk through your new city exhausted.
You can't stay home much since your roommate
has already decided yours is a relationship

of convenience. Wanda is from Oneonta, upstate,
and goes to square dances. Wanda majored in home economics
and wants to marry. You wear vinyl or 1950s housedresses

over stunningly unshaved legs and seldom comb
your hair. You refuse to wear underwear. She has a garden,
for god sakes, you say over the phone when Wanda

isn't there. She sews her own clothes!
And at work, during naptime, the kindergartners know
all your songs, their voices rising from their mats,

stronger on the refrains of all the folk songs you know
about longing, Cole Porter songs about longing, Beatles songs of longing.
After the grilled cheeses or chicken nuggets,

we all should just sleep, you say. *Shhhh.*
You sing, *Blackbird singing in the dead
of night. Take these broken wings and learn to fly.*

All your life you were only waiting for this moment to arrive.
Thin, whispery singing rises again. But they keep
their eyes shut and faces to the floor.

4.

Wanda makes you scrub out the tub after every use. You don't
cook since you can't maintain the cleanliness
she requires. No matter how hard you try, she will,

with a tight look on her face,
say the wooden spoon is stained.
So, at night, four or five times a week, you fall in

love with all the uglier ones at the Thalia. Jimmy Cagney's
small, explosive body in *White Heat*, *look at me Ma,
I'm on top of the world*. Jean Harlowe's pudgy stomach

and unglamorous nose. She was famous
because she'd do anything—look at *Red Dust*, 1931 and she's
naked in the tub. *Gilda*, and you almost can't bear

Rita Hayworth's long curling hair,
quick hips, long limbs. *If I were a ranch, I'd be Bar Nothing*,
Rita growls into the camera. You stumble

from the dark having rehearsed and survived danger
and suffering. You approach these films like an addict, bingeing
on feeling. *Nanook of the North* you watch many times

one Saturday, to see Nanook grin, to see his children
play with knives, their tiny sled, and to see the whole family
finally go to sleep together in a pile of furs.

The original *Nanook* was shot on early,
highly combustible film stock and Robert Flaherty,
a chronic smoker, when editing it, dropped a spark into

the open canister and lost everything. Flaherty returned
to the North, found Nanook, and asked him to recreate
what Flaherty remembered and liked. What you loved was

the notion that Nanook was performing the ordinary.
But unlike you, Nanook has the smile
of someone who is just about to laugh out loud.

You say but there's nothing to be sad about in my life.
You've merely learned actions have consequences.
If you have sex, you can get pregnant. If you don't go to class,

you do not pass, and if you drink too much you get sick.
Why this is such a devastating revelation, you're not sure.
But you mourn this knowledge terribly. What confuses you,

separates you from understanding grief, is
your father, your mother, your sisters, all trigger

a mounting tightness, a pressure behind your eyeballs,
the ache in your windpipe. How could it
be grief when the thought of the living makes you cry?

Dogs don't kill themselves; they live and that's all
they do. You say to yourself, *just decide you want
to live—a leap of faith.* A price of money, of patience,

of pain—what cost to the soul is this enduring.

      5.

Spring in New York is a fabulous thing. You stop worrying
so much about where the homeless can sleep; the trees bloom
within their concrete skirts and chicken wire sleeves.

It is easier to sit on the subway, with no big coats
and muddy boots. Stepping up out of a station into
sun makes a person feel lucky. Sandals start appearing

and those bare toes, tender bones on the city streets are giddy acts
of faith. The wind from the ocean is warm and the few
tulips planted in the meridians of the avenues are nature enough.

Wanda, one afternoon, windows open, curtains roiling on the wind,
announces spring-cleaning. You have to be told
you are expected to participate. Boric acid kills roaches

and Wanda is diligent in battle; the floors look dusty
with it. She arms you with a toothbrush, a nail file,
a pastry brush. Soon the satisfaction of a chore—

that beginning, middle and endness of it—takes over.
Wanda puts on one of her records,
Carly Simon or Billy Joel and you scrub side by side,

announce your achievements or sing along with the music,
you're so vain, I bet you think this song is about you.
Finally, you oil the old wood floors, trap yourselves

on the square of linoleum in the kitchen. Wanda
pulls a couple little green packets from the freezer.
The last of it, she sighs, putting a large pot of water to boil.

No more pesto. What's pesto? you ask at the table, strangely
comfortable with Wanda in the fresh, spring-filled room.
She wonders how good these last couple of bags can be.

She can't wait to grow basil again because, she says,
there's nothing like it. You have walked by
her community garden—an abandoned lot by the housing projects

on Columbus. Vegetable gardens, where you come from,
are too necessary to be sport, but a New York City garden
is more festive—the lot criss-crossed by bright string

and homemade signs announcing each gardener's little square
of earth. When you taste that first bite of pesto,
you cannot believe such a green flavor can exist.

6.

You find a packet of photographs, later
by years. That New York winter, after so many black-and-white
movies, you spent some of your money on a camera.

On weekends, you and your camera
would head over to Central Park and take pictures
of people without asking. A man in a thick coat

and a tall fur hat. A lone bicyclist, an old woman in high heels
feeding birds by the reservoir. Most of the time, however,
you shot photos of shadows, piles of sticks, graffiti. All in New York's

severe, high-contrast winter light. Now you wonder,
what are these images of? These photographs, once perfect expressions
seem boring. Your physical distance from your living

subjects indicates how scared you were, that's what they document,
when you now wish for an image of the kids at school,
naptime, or the igloo city you helped them build

after a snowstorm trapped you all at school. That distance you stood
in your photographs in inverse proportion to the power
this world had to wreck you—but you entered it as one enters

water in the summer, without fear or guile—and the brief glory of the door
flung open, the whoosh of air through the subway car,
the in and through of every suffering you felt fully and well,

this is what you try to recall, organize.

WeatherCam — the Horizon

On the ten o'clock news, the weatherman replays the florid day on a loop
filmed from the top of the News Center Building, plays at super speeds

that whole day. Suppose he played the real one—the man at the Rainbow Mart
singing country with K-BUL, the marrying of ketchups, the polishing of shoes,

the wet rotten leaves pulled from beds of irises in the alleyway,
the news flash from Oklahoma City, the chaos blooming

as we stand at a counter, cross the living room, TV left on
by accident, catch a radio switched from jazz to this undoing,

the newscaster who weeps while she announces: *there are babies*
just unburied, alive, you can claim them at the corner of . . .

the phone call from our husbands, wives, lovers bored
and unaware at work to say that it's too long this day—

no, he shows us the day from the point of view of the WeatherCam,
pointed at the horizon: a narrow cloud or two whizzes by,

the blue shifts in place like a woman who cannot bear her
body, and we are overcome by how even these sterling, western

heavens change, how at dusk the traffic below stills to a bright sluice
as the sun abandons its chase—the skyscrapers, the highways,

the glowing dome of the State House. How at night, at fast-forward,
little changes, a few minor twitches of light, and we begin

to hope the film will keep playing, take us beyond the ten o'clock news,
the rescue dogs and their handlers deplaning, the artist's sketch of a young,

thin, Caucasian man seen leaving a truck, the smaller things that we will
never mention now, take us through to the other edge of the day

where we will see what the weatherman knew all along: the locust
and magnolia flowers, still tender, more bud than bloom, crisp

and dying on a branch's sheath of snow, the skies, again, that forgetful blue.

To Ireland, To Bethlehem

The plane is packed and over sweaty heads,
        rumpled hair, the movie glows in the transatlantic nighttime
     murmur of priests and nuns and Riverdancers returning

home—a baby is cooed by an older mother, a boy feels
        for his seat in the dark. I've read my books
     already, 2 days traveling, the difficulties

technical. *I hate that money*, says the priest beside me,
        and he orders another scotch, his third.
     The Feast of the Epiphany tomorrow, he studies religious

journals for a message, writes in a notebook
        impossibly small. *We are having problems*
   with sound, the flight attendant announces,

it is not your headset, and so the oceans swell in silence,
        bright blue tumbles across the screen mutely, foam
     collapsing over a tiny nimble figure

but she darts through to a green glow,
        sunshine through a veil of wave, her surfboard tense between
     her feet and the world's largest ocean. Her ride

is long, impossibly long—her hips stay low, a friend
              drops onto her wave and, together, they glide towards the shore.
       No music. Just water and that blue. I check the SkyMall catalogue

for something I might need and didn't know. There are
              reasons I am flying over the ocean, reasons I
       I wish I were sure of. Someday I might say, *yes, I chose*

him, and it wasn't wise. Or maybe we'll be old and
              surrounded by our own. The screen flashes;
       the surf is wild, but the bright sky makes me whisper,

Hawaii, where nothing could be that beautiful
              but is. The waves are bigger and she sets out, flowered
       bikini, hair pulled back in a serious bun.

But too soon she's underwater, arms above her head,
              spinning down into a champagne sea.
       The priest asks would I like some English chocolate. I say *no*

at first and then say *yes*. I say,
              how many Euros for the scotch? The baby Jesus
       is about to be adored by black men, foreign kings, in

fact, tomorrow. They're stumbling, the Magi,
              12 days across an ocean and through the desert.
       It's hot so they must travel at night—

who wouldn't? And there was that star, sudden and perhaps a sign.
              We've already tried to get there once,
       I want to say to the kings. It's cool in this 747,

which later the pilot will land with only one engine.
		A problem with
		compressors. But what a sweet,

sweet ocean, and those few younger girls
			who try to ride it. And what a night,
		warmed by the sun-shocked smell

of saddle and sweat, the strong breath of camels.
		What carved, fragrant trunkfuls
		born across deserts and ready to be opened before an infant god.

The Bitter After

A stranger sits in a living room during
a party,
limbs long, rangy like yours
tossed over the back
of the sofa, crossed on each other,
kinetic
through his thin trousers, the
conversation and because
I knew you I know

his sturdy shield of ribs, the leg
thrown over mine
would be wiry even in sleep. Stopped
by the coincidence of his dark lashes, I wish the past,
those days and nights
could have been doubled because I was so happy.

But happy is not
the word for this, maybe,
I want, or ache that animates
the space between me
and the rest of the world.

Once a man gave up flight.

Before he even knew her, he named her
                    Porcelain Cup,
Keyhole, called her shadow
                    Dark One,
              and *Lunar Thirst I Have Found.*

He flew through her
narrow window and the great

                              shadow he cast into her room
              poured into her lap and it had
                    wings.
                    She watched

                              the black sequin
of his eye,
              the scurry of beak and nail.

                    To him, the earth was quick

with vermin, water was a thing
              he could smell and flight

                              broke
the sky into measurable pieces. His ankle
       was banded and his wing
                    bore a small yellow marker. It read,

                              the hawk is the most noble

bird,
              and, *I have loved you for years*, but she watched

                    unmoved.

He beat his wings
       once,

                    closed them like knives to his sides—

Marie says the woman *covered her head in fear*

but I see her face

and it's empty as a bowl

even as his
wings
dissolve, his feet
grow boots, his face a beard.

Once, the voice of god
walked through the garden,
this is after

the snake, after the apple, when we began
our losses that litter
the world.

It was a voice walking on its big legs
towards the human

and what is called
the grief of Adam
begins—the snake must eat dust, bruise

the human heel.

We named it *suffer*—

the wheat from fields full of
thistles—and birth is what the tearing of one
body
from another was called.

We named it *shame*,

when we made clothes.

The voice said,   (hear
the gate, the end and its

wind):

*for dust thou art and unto dust shalt thou
return.*

Why not believe we couldn't trade
                              a garden for this inscrutable desert,
                    obedience for the infinite variety
                                        of pain?
          Did god really think we wouldn't
                              step into desire,

                                             this bitter
                              after? Please
                                        understand the
                              bird who became a
                              man

               —the thought of her
                              arms and the slick of skin
on skin, heavy
                    as milk,
          that mammal hot in the cry
     between, understand
               as she combs her long hair, the idea of her mouth
                                        to his ear sometimes takes
him
back
to that shake
     of feathers, the stagger of flight. You
                              know this grief,
where we must
see the sweet face of the beloved
dry and bloodless
          in every kiss, the pallor of dying,
                    the languor and blue of death

more and more
takes hold of his body. You, I want to say,
            the face that lifts from mine,
                    are already dying, light as leaves, and still

        it's my eyes
my lover closes with his hand, my sheets
        full of ashes.

            Believe me, the woman unmoved
            by the man-bird knows,
            she is the one
                    who has swallowed
the sea, as in the children's story, lets the others—
hands slick
        with scales, boots sucking at the mud—
gather up the panting fish. This
desperate scuttle,
she's decided   (without you)
                                        is not
                    preferable to a solitary Eden. So why
        does she hold out her hands
                to him who's flown through the window
        into her room? How can she say,

my love, it must   be   holy,
            must be wine into blood, and
                    bread into body
                resurrection at the gates of the tomb
        it must be victory, palace, cord.

He stroked her hands,
                said to ask for her nurse, for the priest,

say she feared
she needed
extreme unction
and then
she should hide.

She watched
from behind the heavy drapes.
At the knock on the door, hers
was the body
he had become—him
with her thin jaw, hooded eyes,
taking communion on the tongue,
her feet and head
anointed with chrism
and when everyone left

the man who had been a bird
walked towards her across the room
strewn with other people's grief
and it was her face,
her own voice that walked, that said,
can you believe I love you now?

It is said for each of us
there are two portions—one is what we need to know
for salvation.
This is clearly revealed to us
on earth. The other
is the rest—which may remain
obscured,
doled out, in the pebble in the shoe, the number of crows in
the sky,
or not at all

and there are times now that I'm alone, I believe Marie, believe grief
              is better

                when   I think of a room in Durango, your
              face intense against mine,
                      over my shoulder,
              hands
                  that took off my clothing, your voice—
        look at your long black hair in the mirror,
    look at my eyes, see how beautiful
      we look together.

And then, my body again becomes

                        precious to me and yours
                        becomes mortal.

Sorry I Don't Like You

It's old-fashioned, struggling
with grace. Last night in the movie version
of "Portrait of a Lady," Isabelle will not reveal
that Osmond is cruel. Provoked,

she might, at the most, weep into her hands.
O white skin and narrow
fingers lit by tears, all that money
was supposed to set you free.

Those days it was enough to worry
about marriage—it was fate. End up
with an Osmond and the rest of your life
equaled grief and its awful seductions.

These days marriage's not enough
so this world delivers
lessons everywhere about humility.
The doctor sends sound waves,

dyes, and tubes into you. A benign tumor
is measured, your car fills with rain, a neighbor
asks for money.
There's a dark night and the edge

of what you feel is possible, a call
to grace while the days give up their
black yolks, the smudge that opens up
nothing so dramatic as not living,

only the likelihood of doing without.
The landscape shimmers with
fear. You try to stay unemphatic.
The oleanders are blooming

and heavy with hummingbirds
and you should not have, ten years ago, done
all those things which leave you
hands empty now. On a Zen tape, the master says,

when I was young I was a tiger
and now I am a cat. It is better to be a cat.
I think of the brutal tiger,
the slung hips and thumping tail,

the coiled rump, that mouth.
I think of my ex-cat, neat whiskers
patient at the door. What glamour,
the tiger in all its teeth. I think I have

made a mess. I was reading
some poems, a series addressed
to the poet's friend who fell into a coma
while traveling in China, one from which

he never awoke. The poems are
about kindness: the times they carried his body
to the garden to sleep in the trees, the music
they played and the stories they told

what was left of a man named Steve.
They are poems I cannot recall without weeping
because if I were to stop living now—what regret
I feel. It soaks me like a fog

imperceptibly heavier each day. The burden,
what I should have done better, the opportunities
I pissed away, like Isabelle Archer, given fortune
(of a sort), beautiful youth

and desire. Am I Isabelle Osmond
who now knows better as she kisses
her dying cousin? Maybe regret is the final rebellion
of the puny, the only grace we can manage,

the edge we worry between despair and stepping
through. Maybe *I should not have done it* is how
we can say to the ways things are now
sorry, I don't like you.

The Beginning of Things

for Rus

Your west each
                morning
        gives doves—night

dissolved by torrents of
                sun
        and of doves—a

constant coo, coo
                stretches into
        your room. Here, no easy

song. Melody,
                with its grace-
        note skitterings above

avoids these empty (rusted blades
                of a windmill,
        a radio tower, browned peak)

skies. *It's only*
                doves, and you pull
        towards my back,

pull back towards
              sleep where you don't,
        you tell me, dream. I doubt

daily—though here's
              heat, body, the weakness
        (giving in) to your scratch

and pitch, voice. *Flesh*
              is grass. Rare
        high meadow of which I

might dream?
              Or meaning everywhere,
        like the ache

of miles of desert, the beaten
              armor of mountain? And doves
        insisting, wherever

they are. Waves of alto and the
              blue square of window holds
        nothing tangible

again: flat light, jets
              evaporating into
        white, heat that stands

like a man with a sword,
              this sudden need
        for belief. My new love.

Soon you won't
　　　　even hear them. White
　　noise, you said and still

I listen. I hear
　　　　a steady
　　question, who?

Who are you,
　　　　narrow stranger? *Trust me*,
　　you said one night,

swung a heavy stick
　　　　into the hive-shaped tree,
　　they're in there.

And dark bodies
　　　　flew upward
　　a hundred in one teeming cloud.

This is for the silver of highway

through Iowa, Nebraska, Wyoming, for
the idea of open road, how it makes of the world
a *camera lucida*—a timeless, illuminated room.

The psalmist felt this shine, wrote the womb
of the morning, wrote *the mountains skipped like rams,*
and the little hills like lambs. David Copperfield

begins tenderly, his voice earnest on the first
of eight tapes of the BBC radio play,
announces his desire to tell us the journey

of his life, while one October, in Wyoming,
herds of black cows turn into mythical animals
because they are black and shiny and stand head to toe,

bodies fusing in the bright sun, one tar-black body
with two opposing heads. Tar, tarmac, macadam,
asphalt, highway, freeway, interstate,

scenic byway while Copperfield is rescued
over and over by ignorance and luck combined with
his own good soul. *Where am I?* I ask gas station

attendant, cashier, hotel clerk. One August through
Ohio, I sweat up the steering wheel, seat, lay bags of ice
across my lap, hurtle past exploded tires,

wild anemone of wire and rind. *You torrent,*
you headstrong, they whisper. September, an Iowa rest stop
hours from anywhere, I watch a man unload

a lawnmower from his truck, the motor vivid
in the quiet air as he begins to cut the grass around the latrines.
A congregation of small, brown birds lifts

from the bushes as if of one mind and my body trills
with that highway feeling, of feeling the world
and mind are one. It's a giddy amnesia—history,

responsibility lose their dominion in February, in Nevada hills
mute with sage. It's religious how I remember
July, the air-conditioned relief of the Chicago Art Institute,

where grimy, the road still droning in my arms, my chest,
my inner ear, I want to explain to the becalmed tourists
the velocity of Whistler—the twisted, crossing, intersecting

lines of sight from boatman, wavetip, to wingtip,
to fin. I return to my car and navigate acres
of backhoes, dumptrucks, a massive construction

site ringing the hogbutcher to the world.
One June I get a speeding ticket in Pennsylvania
because the radio's playing an optimistic song

from the 1970s while the speed limit changes
and I am watching instead a farmer harness up
two golden draft horses, pull them right

to the porch of his house and a bonneted woman
emerges to admire them. I admire them.
Where am I? In a motel in Cheyenne,

filled with school kids and their band
instruments and the mountains are green,
because this time it's early, it's May, and David Copperfield

has lost both women he loved, two weak, incompetent
women and still I cry—this is how it happens,
passion and its unreasonable vaults of soul

and what fills me are miles and David's sad love
and the plain face of a girl holding a trumpet
on a Super 8 Motel balcony in Wyoming.

Where am I? The stuff of my life in boxes, thrown out,
whittled to a few books, a computer and some clothes.
I think I am suffering, but I don't know. Here's to

not where I'm coming from and not where I'm going.
Here's to gypsy movement (as my grandmother
calls it), the infinity of living between.

Notes

"The Bird is Her Reason," "Apart, Away," and "The Bitter After" are adaptations of Marie de France's *lais*, specifically, "Chevrefoil," "Laustic," and "Yonec."

"The Bitter After"—I have stolen a line from Sappho in this poem, "I wish those days and nights could have been doubled because I was so happy." The line "the ache that animates the space" is adapted from an interview with Ann Lauterbach. I also owe thanks to Julian of Norwich in the section describing the death of the beloved.

"Anonymous Lyric"—the quotations in this poem are from anonymous sixteenth-century love lyrics and from "Night Fever" by the Bee Gees.

"Dangerous for Girls"—Chandra Levy's remains were eventually discovered in a park in Washington, D.C. in 2002, her murder unsolved. Aileen Wuarnos was executed by lethal injection in 2002. The mother of the five boys in Texas, Andrea Yates, who was serving a life sentence, was recently granted another trial.

"To Ireland, To Bethlehem"—the surfing movie mentioned is *Blue Crush*.

"Sorry I Don't Like You"—the poet mentioned is El Paso poet Bobby Byrd.

"This is for the silver of highway"—I thank Robert Landon who witnessed route 80 with me once. Also, the mythical animal mentioned is a Push-Me Pull-You from Hugh Lofting's *Dr. Doolittle*. The *camera lucida* mentioned is from Roland Barthes' book of the same name.